Jamaica

Michael Capek

🌿 Carolrhoda Books, Inc. / Minneapolis

Photo Acknowledgments

Photos, maps, and artworks are used courtesy of: John Erste, pp. 1, 2–3, 10–11, 20–21, 24–25, 27 (bottom), 30 (bottom, top right), 36, 37; © Stephen Graham Photography, pp. 4, 14, 18 (top), 26 (left), 38; Laura Westlund, pp. 5, 23; © Robert Fried/Robert Fried Photography, pp. 6, 7 (top), 8, 31, 33 (bottom); **Photo Network:** (© Mark Sherman) p. 7 (bottom), (© Todd Powell) pp. 15 (bottom), 16, (© Jeff Greenberg) p. 20; Jamaica Tourist Board, pp. 9, 10, 24, 34, 35; **Visuals Unlimited:** (© Jeff Greenberg) pp. 12, 39, 45, (© Max & Bea Hunn) p. 44; Jim Simondet, p. 13; © Buddy Mays/Travel Stock Photography, pp. 15 (top), 26 (right), 33 (top); **Bruce Coleman, Inc.:** (© Guido Cozzi) pp. 17, 22–23, (© Tony Arruza) pp. 18 (bottom), 40, (© Elisa Leonelli) pp. 41, 43; © John and Penny Hubley, from the title *Jamaican Village*, A & C Black (Publishers) Limited, London, p. 19; Astor, Lenox, and Tilden Foundations, New York Public Library Rare Book Division, p. 27 (top); **© Trip:** (D. Saunders) p. 28, (R. Graham) p. 29; © W. Lynn Seldon, Jr., pp. 30 (top left), 42 (both); © Joan Iaconetti, p. 32. Cover photo of boats at Ocho Rios, Jamaica, © W. Lynn Seldon, Jr.

Carolrhoda Books, Inc.
c/o The Lerner Publishing Group
241 First Avenue North
Minneapolis, Minnesota 55401 U.S.A.

Website address: www.lernerbooks.com

Words in **bold type** are explained in a glossary that begins on page 44.

Library of Congress Cataloging-in-Publication Data

Capek, Michael.
    Jamaica / by Michael Capek.
        p. cm. — (Globe-trotters club)
    Includes index.
    Summary: An overview of Jamaica emphasizing its cultural aspects.
    ISBN 1–57505–112–5 (lin. bdg. : alk. paper)
    1. Jamaica—Juvenile literature. [1. Jamaica.] I. Title. II. Series:
Globe-trotters club (Series)
F1868.2.C36 1999
972.92—DC21.   97–8739

Manufactured in the United States of America
1 2 3 4 5 6 – JR – 04 03 02 01 00 99

Contents

White, sandy beaches and clear, turquoise water make up large parts of Jamaica's coastline. Other parts are sheer cliffs.

Welcome to **Jamaica, Mon!**

 It's easy to find Jamaica on a map. Off the southern tip of Florida, find the island nation of Cuba. It looks a little bit like a dolphin. Now find the island below Cuba. That's Jamaica!

Jamaica rises from the Caribbean Sea, which is part of the Atlantic Ocean. To the south sits South America. Northward is the continent of North America. Central America lies to the west. Islands sit to the east and to the north. Together with Jamaica, these islands are known as the **West Indies.**

Jamaica is 146 miles long and 50 miles wide at its biggest points. That makes it the third largest island in the Caribbean Sea.

Jamaica sits a little to the north of the **equator,** so it's hot year round. Banana plants and coconut palms are a few of the plants that keep the **tropical** island green all year.

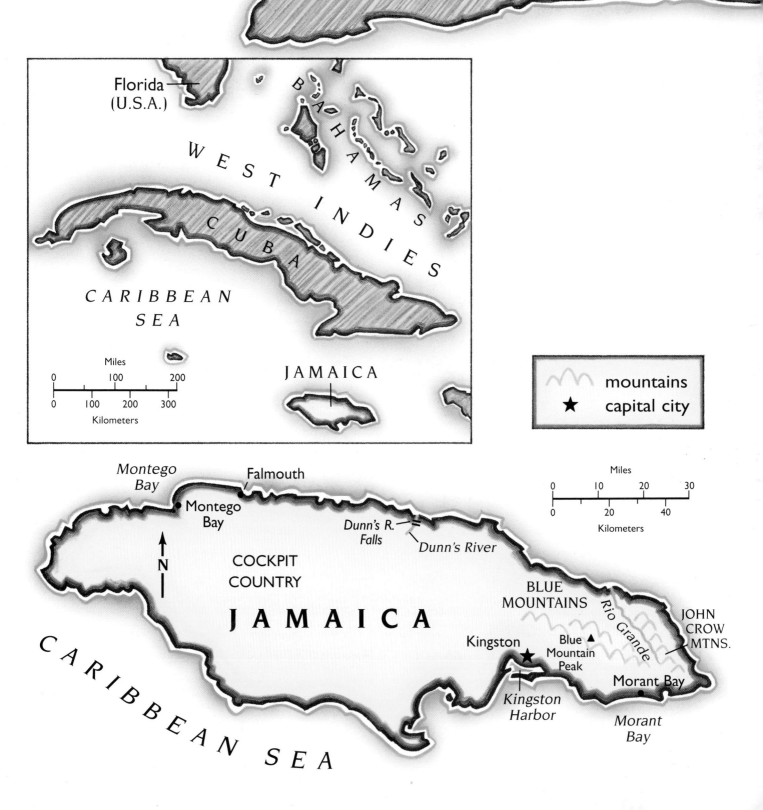

CUBA

Florida
(U.S.A.)

WEST INDIES

BAHAMAS

CUBA

CARIBBEAN
SEA

Miles
0   100   200
0   100   200   300
Kilometers

JAMAICA

⌢⌢⌢ mountains
★ capital city

Montego
Bay

Falmouth

Montego
Bay

Dunn's R.
Falls

Dunn's River

COCKPIT
COUNTRY

BLUE
MOUNTAINS

Rio Grande

JOHN
CROW
MTNS.

JAMAICA

Kingston

Blue ▲
Mountain
Peak

Morant Bay

N

Kingston
Harbor

Morant
Bay

CARIBBEAN SEA

Miles
0   10   20   30
0   20   40
Kilometers

Divers can enjoy the brilliant colors of coral reefs near Jamaica's coast.

Water **Everywhere**

A coral reef surrounds Jamaica like a rainbow-colored, underwater necklace. For centuries the reef has built up the island's coasts and has provided a habitat for sea creatures like tropical fish and moray eels.

Water cuts through Jamaica, too. So it's not unusual to hear the roar of water rushing across the country. More than 120 waterways, such as the Rio Grande and Dunn's River, run through the country. Water even flows through underground caves.

Jamaicans take advantage of all that water. Coastal towns, like Falmouth and Morant Bay, have busy ports. Fishing crews haul in freshly caught seafood. And sparkling waterfalls, like Dunn's River Falls, are favorite spots for kids to play.

Tourists and locals alike enjoy wading and bathing in Dunn's River Falls. Sometimes lines of people join hands and climb the falls in single file. Don't slip!

Finger Food

River rafters might spot one of Jamaica's endangered animals, the American crocodile. Jamaican fisherfolk think of the crocs as gentle. The big reptiles will come right up to the shore or float next to rafts and let people touch them. It's not a good idea to pet a crocodile, though. A nearsighted croc could mistake a hand for a snack and—snap!

This Jamaican home nestles on a peak in the Blue Mountains.

All Across the **Land**

Although Jamaica is flat along the coast, hills and mountains spike the island's inland areas. The John Crow Mountains and the Blue Mountains span most of the eastern third of the island. The Blue Mountains rise to a mountain pine forest that gives way to a misty woodland, where twisted trees hanging with moss and ferns grow. The tallest of these mountains, Blue Mountain Peak, pokes into the clouds. On clear days, mountain climbers can look across the Caribbean Sea and see the island of Cuba—that's a 90-mile view!

Fast Facts about Jamaica

Name: Jamaica
Area: 4,223 square miles
Main Landforms: Blue Mountains, Cockpit Country, John Crow Mountains
Highest Point: Blue Mountain Peak (7,388 feet)
Lowest Point: Sea level
Animals: American crocodile, manatee, doctor bird
Capital City: Kingston
Other Cities: Morant Bay, Montego Bay, Falmouth
Official Language: English
Money Unit: Jamaican dollar

West of the Blue Mountains stretch rugged hills and **plateaus.** A section of **limestone** plateau, called Cockpit Country, is scarred with deep caves, lumpy hills, and gorges. Cockpit Country is beautiful, but hardly anyone lives there. The hills are too bumpy to have farms on them.

Very few roads cross the 500 square miles that make up Cockpit Country.

How's the Weather?

Winter, spring, summer, and fall—they all feel the same in Jamaica! The weather is almost always warm and humid. Temperatures stay around 80 degrees almost everywhere. Even on the highest mountain peaks, the temperature rarely drops below 40 degrees. Jamaica has a rainy season. Most rain falls in September, October, and November.

Jamaica's forecast often calls for sunny weather.

The Most Wicked City on Earth

During the late 1600s, pirates sailed the Caribbean Sea. Many used the Jamaican city of Port Royal at the mouth of Kingston Harbor as a home base, leading some people to call it the "most wicked city on earth." Folks predicted that Port Royal would be swept into the ocean as punishment. And they were right! In 1692 an earthquake swallowed most of the city and caused gigantic waves to surge ashore. Most of Port Royal dropped to the bottom of the sea. Divers later spotted traces of the old town. Archaeologists are still uncovering buildings buried in the ocean floor.

The cool, refreshing **trade winds** carry some of the rains. The winds blow across the island from the northeast and hit the Blue Mountains. Each year the northeastern end of the island receives more than 100 inches of rain. Kingston—on the other side of the Blue Mountains—gets about 30 inches annually.

In late summer and in the fall, **hurricanes** threaten Jamaica. When Hurricane Gilbert struck the island in 1988, the high winds killed many people and ruined homes. Winds even uprooted crops and blew them out to sea. But storms like Gilbert are rare. Most pass by without doing much harm.

11

This plantation house, built in 1881, contains its original furniture and decorations. Modern-day Jamaicans preserve the house as a reminder of their history.

Early **Jamaicans**

Arawak Indians from South America settled on the island, making it their home for hundreds of years. The name Jamaica comes from the Arawak's name for the island, Xamayca, which most linguists believe means "land of wood and water."

Spaniards arrived in the 1500s and forced the Arawak into slavery. When most Arawak people died from abuse, overwork, and diseases, the Spaniards brought Africans to Jamaica as slaves. In the 1600s, England gained control of the island, importing even more slaves.

The slaves worked hard! They built roads, constructed city buildings, shored up harbors, and carved plantations (large farms) out of the forests and rugged hillsides. Life was tough. Slave owners sold children away from parents as soon as the youngsters were old enough to work. Some slaves escaped and banded together in Jamaica's mountains. The escapees, known as Maroons, were fierce fighters and declared war on slaveholders. In 1739, after nearly 40 years of fighting, the British governor offered the Maroons a peace treaty and mountain land on which to live.

In 1834 Britain freed the slaves in all of its **colonies,** but hard times continued. Former slaves fled the plantations for little farms in the hills. Without slave labor, most sugar plantations became too expensive to run.

In 1962 Britain granted Jamaica's independence. Jamaicans designed a new flag to mark the event. Green represents Jamaica's farms and its hope for the future. Black triangles stand for Jamaica's past and for its ties to Africa. Yellow stripes remind Jamaicans of the bright sun.

Out of Many,
One People

A Jamaican man strolls down a beach with his visiting friend. Long ago his ancestors were also newcomers to the island.

 Jamaica's motto is "Out of many, one people." Why? Because the **ancestors** of modern Jamaicans came to the island from across the world.

More than 2.5 million people live in Jamaica. Almost 95 percent have ancestors from the continent of Africa. Most were slaves that the Spaniards and British brought to the island to work on sugarcane plantations in the 1600s, 1700s, and 1800s. Folks from all across Africa brought different languages, folktales, music, cultures, and beliefs to Jamaica. African ways eventually merged with

14

the Ibo, the Mandingo, the Fula, the Yoruba, and the Ashanti.

This bicyclist (below) **and this young farmboy** (right) **both live in Jamaica, but their ancestors may have come from opposite ends of Africa, from India, or from Europe.**

Spanish and British ways to create a new Jamaican culture. After the slaves were freed, **immigrants** from Europe, Africa, and India arrived to take low-paying jobs on plantations. These newcomers added their customs to the island's cultural mix. Over time, folks of different ethnic backgrounds have married one another.

15

Bangarang **Town**

Kingston features a large natural harbor.

Kingston, Jamaica's crowded capital city, is home to one-third of the islanders. It fills the space between the Blue Mountains and the ocean, and it sports a beautiful port. Taxis and buses honk and sputter, while music blares on every corner. Jamaicans use the word *bangarang* to describe the city's noise. Pet dogs, cats, and pigs roam Kingston's zigzagging streets.

Brightly painted apartment houses snuggle up to restaurants, churches, and shops. Some neighborhoods have new high-rise office buildings, while others have older structures from the British colonial days.

Each Kingston neighborhood has its own character. Tivoli Gardens on the west side of Kingston is a low-income community. Its citizens paint every available wall and sidewalk with colorful murals that celebrate Jamaica's history, music, and people. Wealthy neighborhoods in Kingston's outskirts have large homes, swimming pools, and fancy shopping malls.

Folks from rural villages often move to Kingston looking for work. Most end up unemployed and living in dangerous **shantytowns** on the edges of the city.

A busy corner in Kingston bustles with foot traffic.

Family **Matters**

Families in Jamaica are often large, and the members like to help each other out. Folks usually live near their parents, brothers, sisters, aunts, and uncles. Moms are in charge of raising the kids, but they count on aunts, grandmas, and friends to pitch in.

A mother watches her children in the yard of their home (left). **This aunt** (above) **will help to raise her young niece.**

A Jamaican Boy

Meet Martin Samuels. With his family, he lives in a little village named Cascade. His family lives on a farm where they grow **breadfruit,** yams, and other fruits and vegetables. For most of the day, Martin attends grammar school. After school he earns extra cash by running errands. His cart has lights, bumpers, and a steering wheel.

Dads often live far away and only come back to visit a few times a year. Some men leave their families to work as miners in the mountains. Others even travel to another country, such as Canada, where there are more jobs than there are in Jamaica. They help their families by sending money home.

Work **Days**

Most Jamaicans live in the countryside, where some men work in the bauxite mines located in the mountains. Bauxite is used to make aluminum, a lightweight metal. Others work on large sugarcane plantations where some Jamaicans harvest the tough stalks by hand.

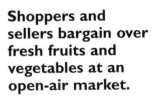

Shoppers and sellers bargain over fresh fruits and vegetables at an open-air market.

Jamaica's mountainous, rocky land makes farming tough. But just about every rural family has a little plot of land. Folks grow yams and breadfruit in the plateau areas. Higher in the mountains, farmers grow coffee beans and strawberries. After feeding their families, farmers bring their extra goods to huge open-air markets, where they sell or barter (trade) food.

Offices and factories employ some cityfolk, but many people work in hotels, restaurants, or stores visited by international tourists. Some women set up shop by spreading goods right on the sidewalks of Jamaica's big towns and cities. Folks call these sellers higglers because, in Jamaica, *higgling* means bargaining over prices. And higglers are experts at bargaining with customers. Higglers hawk different manufactured and handmade Jamaican goods such as straw hats, wood carvings, and woven baskets.

Pardon My
Patois

The official language of Jamaica is English. But **patois** is heard most often in the streets and in homes. Jamaican patois has its own musical sound and vocabulary.

Most patois words are taken from the English language. But others come from Arawak, French, Spanish, or African tongues. Jamaicans put these words together and pronounce them in a Jamaican way. A Jamaican might tell you, "Me donkey sleep," (My donkey is sleeping) or "She go fe to look fe her madda" (She went to look for her mother). Farmers might "go a grung" (go work in the fields).

Patois may sound strange at first, but close listeners can figure out many of the words.

Whether talking face to face or over the phone, Jamaicans usually speak to each other in patois—the Jamaican way of speaking English.

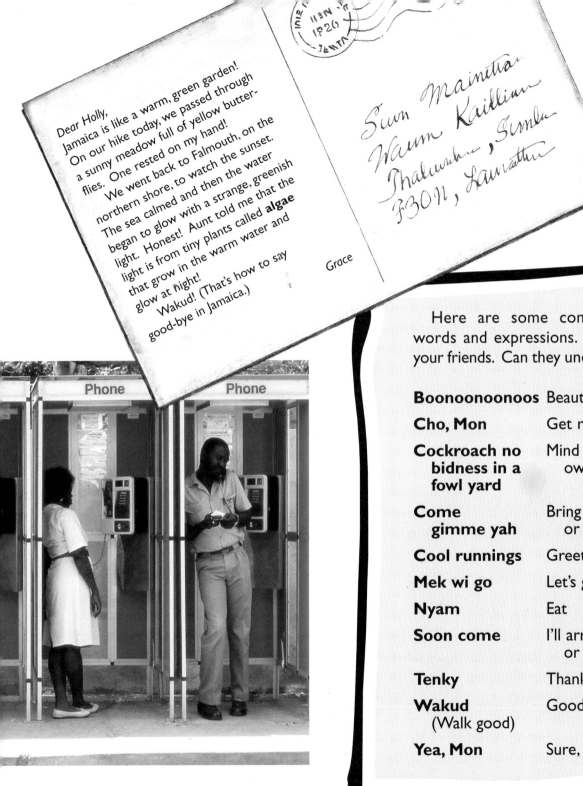

Dear Holly,
Jamaica is like a warm, green garden!
On our hike today, we passed through a sunny meadow full of yellow butter-flies. One rested on my hand!
We went back to Falmouth, on the northern shore, to watch the sunset. The sea calmed and then the water began to glow with a strange, greenish light. Honest! Aunt told me that the light is from tiny plants called **algae** that grow in the warm water and glow at night!
Wakud! (That's how to say good-bye in Jamaica.)

Grace

Here are some common patois words and expressions. Say them to your friends. Can they understand you?

Boonoonoonoos	Beautiful
Cho, Mon	Get real!
Cockroach no bidness in a fowl yard	Mind your own business
Come gimme yah	Bring it here or Give it to me
Cool runnings	Greetings
Mek wi go	Let's go
Nyam	Eat
Soon come	I'll arrive sooner or later
Tenky	Thank you
Wakud (Walk good)	Good-bye
Yea, Mon	Sure, Okay

Let's Celebrate!

Jamaicans love to celebrate! A favorite holiday falls on August 6—the date on which the British government granted Jamaica the right to govern itself. The weeks before Independence Day, called Festival, are busy with competitions in art, music, literature, dance, and drama. For months in advance, students practice to compete or to put on plays. Speeches, historical reenactments, and special ceremonies mark the holiday.

In August Reggae Sunsplash celebrates Jamaican music. Three days of concerts and parties draw **reggae** fans from across the island and from around the world. Famous musicians and beginners come to play.

These dancers are costumed for Jonkonnu, a celebration that comes shortly before Christmas.

Most Jamaicans celebrate religious holidays with special traditions. Jonkonnu, a Christmas festival, dates from the days of slavery. Nobody knows for sure who or what Jonkonnu is supposed to be. The festival probably came from Africa. Masked merrymakers, singers, dancers, and drummers parade through Jamaican villages. Participants wear masks that look like the heads of horses and other farm animals. The character of John Canoe (another way to say Jonkonnu) wears a mixed-up costume—he might have the tusks of a wild boar, a sword, and a cow's tail.

A Jonkonnu Song

In past times, dancers collected money from onlookers to help pay for their Christmas celebration. A song traditionally sung by the dancers draws attention to the fact that they needed money to buy gifts (lama) and fine clothes (deggeday).

Christmas a come,
me wun me lama,
Christmas a come,
me wun me lama,
Christmas a come,
me wun me deggeday
Christmas a come,
me wun me deggeday.

Soon **Come!**

Getting from place to place in Jamaica can be tough. Few families own cars. Although taxis crowd city streets, they are too expensive for most people to use. Jamaicans often choose eye-popping purple and red buses to take them where they need to go. But buses are jam-packed with riders and take their own time to get places. Jamaicans are used to being early or late. "Soon come!" is a popular Jamaican expression that means, "Sooner or later! We'll get there sometime!"

If you want to get from place to place in Jamaica, there are many ways to go. A bamboo raft could take you down a river (above). **Or you could hop on a bike** (left) **and pedal away.**

Boats are a convenient and cheap way to travel Jamaica's waterways. Most folks can easily make a raft by using vines to tie together a dozen or so long bamboo poles. The rafts slowly drift down the rivers.

26

Pirates

Anne Bonny and Mary Read were two of Jamaica's toughest pirates.

These days boats safely cruise the Caribbean. But in the 1700s, no trading ship in the sea was safe from pirates for whom Jamaica was a favorite hangout. Their cruelty and greed became legendary. Some were just crazy! Edward Teach, known as Blackbeard, used to tie lighted fuses in his hair and beard before he attacked. His blazing head was a scary sight. Anne Bonny and Mary Read were pirates on the ship of "Calico Jack" Rackham. After a furious battle in the 1720s, the English captured Rackham's ship. Mary and Anne were the last two pirates still alive and fighting! Both were eventually taken to jail in England.

Crazy for **Cricket**

Jamaicans are crazy for cricket, their national sport. Introduced by the British, cricket is kind of like baseball, but it's more complicated. Instead of bases, cricket has two wickets. From one of the wickets, a player pitches a small, hard ball toward a batsman (a batter), who stands in front of the other wicket. The batsman tries to hit the ball with a flat wooden bat. If the batsman hits the ball, the player runs between the wickets to score points.

Jamaica's teams play folks from other Caribbean islands. A team with players from many West Indian nations competes with teams from Britain, Pakistan, Australia, and other cricket-loving countries.

Jamaican fans celebrate every play with wild cheering, singing, dancing, and drumming. A test match (a tournament involving a number of teams) can bring regular business to a halt as everybody listens to the games over the radio. Matches go on for hours or even days.

Cricket is a game most Jamaicans just watch. But everybody plays dominoes! In parks, schools, and cafés, noisy groups crowd around stacks of dominoes. Jamaicans also enjoy tennis, boxing, golf, swimming, and scuba diving. Track and field events are popular, too. Some runners even become Olympic medalists, including Merlene Ottey who took home two silver medals in the 1990 Olympics.

Way to Go!

It doesn't snow in Jamaica—not even on mountaintops. But that didn't stop some Jamaicans. In 1988 Jamaica sent a four-person bobsled team to the winter Olympics. The athletes and their coaches had their share of spills and didn't win a medal, but the team members impressed fans from all over the world with their determination and courage. Do your best and have fun—that's the Jamaican way.

A boy takes a mighty swing at the ball in a back-alley cricket match.

A Kingston student is ready for the day's lessons.

Time for **School**

Lots of kids go to school in Jamaica. To give youngsters some elbow room, students go to school in shifts. Some kids might attend an early shift from 7 A.M. until noon, while others chose the later shift, from about 1 P.M. until 5 P.M. This system cuts the number of kids in each class, but students might still have to share textbooks with their classmates.

Most Jamaican kids between the ages of 6 and 15 go to school. At the age of 10, children take tests that determine their next step. A high test score might mean that a kid gets to attend an excellent high school. Others might enroll in comprehensive schools, which are like junior high. Some leave school to work.

At the age of 15 or 16, students take tests that place them in one of many different programs. Lots of kids choose to learn a trade such as metalwork, welding, carpentry, or farming. Some teenagers go on to college, but most try to find jobs instead. Few Jamaicans have an education beyond the high school level.

A typically large class of elementary school students gathers in a hallway.

These girls wear uniforms at their church-run elementary school.

Dress **Cool!**

The weather has a lot to do with what people wear in Jamaica. Jamaicans like bright colors or patterns, but many choose to wear white because it reflects the glaring sun, keeping them cooler in hot weather. Many women wear dresses, and men often put on long pants and shirts, even in hot weather. Lots of grown-ups top things off with a hat every day. Men favor floppy woolen tams (a flat, knitted hat). When dressing up, women like fancy sun hats with broad, floppy brims that help shield their faces from the hot sun. On other days, most women choose kerchiefs. Girls might do their hair in fancy braids that help keep them cool, and most boys wear their hair very short.

A light-colored dress and kerchief will help this woman stay cool in the hot sun (left). **This man is wearing a tam** (below).

Children normally sport shorts or swimsuits. But on school days, most Jamaican kids put on uniforms. Girls wear skirts or jumpers of blue, green, brown, or gray. Boys have tan or blue uniforms with epaulets (cloth decorations on the shoulders). Different schools usually have different stripes or markings on the epaulets. Jamaican kids wear starched (stiff) white shirts under their uniforms. Some uniforms include neckties.

Art **All Over**

An artist shows a
self-portrait that he
has carved in wood.

Art has a long history in Jamaica. In ancient times, the Arawak Indians painted on the walls of caves and sculpted wooden figures called zemis. Early Jamaican artists believed that their works should look like European art. But that idea changed in the 1940s.

Edna Manley, a sculptor, made beautiful wood carvings inspired by Jamaican subjects such as island animals and people. She believed that the island's artists should create works that reflect Jamaican culture. Edna Manley helped found an art school in the 1940s that taught lots of Jamaican artists to be proud of their own heritage.

Kingston is full of museums and theatres. Audiences love to watch the National Dance Theatre Company of Jamaica perform African-influenced dances.

This painting shows Jamaican people doing everyday things, such as playing drums or sleeping.

Anancy **Stories**

Jamaicans love to listen to stories. Speaking in patois, dub poets give riveting performances of traditional tales, folk songs, and new poems about Jamaican life. Dub poetry has strong rhythms that listeners echo as they shout, clap, or drum along with the performer.

Some dub poetry performances tell stories of Anancy, a magical spider. According to the stories, Anancy is older than humankind—even older than the world itself! In fables about Anancy, the spider always tricks other animals. He hates it when animals brag or show off, so many of the stories show him punishing animals with mean tricks. Sometimes his tricky ways get him into lots of trouble. But Anancy is so clever that he always manages to get himself out again. Most Anancy folktales provide fanciful explanations of why the world works the way it does.

The Great Race

One time Anancy and Donkey were arguing over who was fastest, Donkey or Toad. Anancy bet Donkey that Toad could outrun him. Early on the day of the race, Anancy brought Toad and his 50 children to the racecourse, where he stationed the toads along the grassy path.

During the race, when one toad got tired, another hopped out of the grass and took up the race. Because they all looked exactly alike, Donkey couldn't tell the difference. No matter how hard he ran, he always saw a toad hopping ahead of him! Of course, he lost. Donkey never discovered Anancy's trick. He was so ashamed that he hung his head and vowed never to race again.

That's why Donkey hangs his head sadly to this day and why he always takes things slow and easy.

Folklorists believe that Anancy stories originated among the Ashanti, a people living in what would become the African nation of Ghana. Many Jamaicans trace their heritage to Ghana.

The Beat
Goes On

Slaves brought drums with them from Africa. At first they were allowed to beat traditional rhythms. When slave owners realized that the drumming was a way of communicating, the owners forbade it. But the slaves continued to play music and to sing in secret. Slaves adopted European instruments, including the fiddle, and learned many English songs. Often, slaves sang as they worked.

A musician entertains customers at a small restaurant.

Bob Marley

The most famous reggae musician was Bob Marley. His songs brought so much attention to his country that he was awarded the Jamaican Order of Merit—the highest honor the nation gives its citizens. When Marley died in 1981, the line of funeral mourners stretched for 55 miles! Fans put up a statue of the singer in front of his house, which became a museum.

Mento was a popular music style in the early and mid-twentieth century. Slow, sad songs—sometimes adapted from sailors' sea chants—were accompanied by guitar playing and bongo drumming. *Ska* became popular in the early 1960s. Most ska music has happy lyrics and a cheerful beat. In the late 1960s, Jamaican musicians began to write songs with thought-provoking lyrics. Named reggae, this music has a steady beat that musicians adapted from African drumming. Players strum electric guitars. Reggae music's rich sound and peaceful message have become popular all over the world.

Rap music has Jamaican origins, too. Singers mixed their own words over recorded music, often using rhythms from dub poetry. Some dub poets recite, rap, or sing while reggae bands perform or while records play.

Women, wearing their best Sunday clothes, walk home from a Christian religious service.

Religious
Beliefs

The British and Spanish colonists brought Christianity to Jamaica, where many African slaves began to practice the religion. These days, most Jamaicans are Christians. Many people get dressed up and walk to church on Sundays. Other folks follow belief systems with African roots, such as Obeah and Pocomania. Some Jamaicans combine belief systems.

Rastafarianism is probably the most noticable religion in Jamaica. Most Rastafarians are easy to spot because they do not cut their hair. Instead, they wear it in long, matted twists called dreadlocks. Dreadlocks are supposed to look like the lion's shaggy mane, a Rasta symbol. The ropelike locks are sometimes tucked up under a tam. Rastafarians worship the former emperor of Ethiopia, Haile Selassie, and many are in favor of moving to the African lands of their ancestors. Others want to help the poor people in Jamaica.

There aren't many Rastafarians, but they have a big impact on Jamaican culture. Rastas have a lot of pride in themselves, which has given many other people a new sense of pride in being Jamaican. Many reggae musicians, including Bob Marley, were Rastafarians.

Rastafarians wear their hair in long dreadlocks.

Whoo, that's good! A woman serves herself a plate of food (left). **This basket of akee** (right) **is ripe and ready to cook.**

Let's **Nyam!**

Nyam! Remember that word? It's patois for eat. Salt fish (salted cod) with akee is the most popular Jamaican meal. Akee is a yellow-golden fruit with a reddish blush. Watch out! Unripe akee is poisonous. Jamaicans know that as soon as the fruit pops open to show its large seeds, it's safe to eat. Cooked akee looks like scrambled eggs. Jamaicans love akee for breakfast!

Jamaicans also enjoy other fruits and seafoods. Luckily, the island has lots of both. One popular dish is mackerel rung-dung, which is made by cooking a mackerel with coconut milk, tomatoes, onions, and a lot of hot red peppers. The gooey, delicious stew is served with a helping of boiled green bananas, yams, and bammies (flat round pancakes).

Another popular Jamaican dish is jerk pork or chicken. The word *jerk* refers to the special blend of spices and herbs used to flavor the meat.

Islanders sip plenty of drinks. One popular beverage is made from sorrel, a dark red, leafy vegetable sold across Jamaica. Kids love to eat green coconuts, called jellies. They drink the juice and eat the fruit.

Barbacoa!

Long ago Jamaicans cooked whole pigs or chickens in a pit filled with red-hot coals. They coated the meat with a mixture of lime juice, hot peppers, and native spices. They called the cooking method barbacoa. Sound familiar?

Few modern Jamaicans barbecue in pits in the ground. Some use modern grills. Many make their own grills out of clean, empty oil drums. In Jamaican cities and towns, it's easy to spot the thick smoke rising from barbecue stalls. Boonoonoonoos! De best!

Glossary

algae: Plants without roots, stems, or leaves that grow in large groups in water.

ancestor: A relative in the past, such as a great-great-great grandparent.

breadfruit: A fruit that, when baked, has a breadlike taste and texture.

colony: A territory ruled by a country that is located far away.

equator: The line that circles a globe's middle section halfway between the North Pole and the South Pole.

hurricane: A windstorm that begins over the ocean, picks up large amounts of rain, and can cause severe damage when striking land.

immigrant: A person who moves from his or her home country to another country.

A farmworker uses a large knife to cut sugarcane stalks.

Dressed in an outfit made of coconut palm leaves, a coconut seller slices his wares for a customer to sample.

limestone: A kind of rock created when shells or coral have been compressed for thousands of years.

patois: A way of speaking a language that is different from the standard way.

plateau: A large area of high, level land.

reggae: A popular style of music that originated in Jamaica.

shantytown: A poor neighborhood with makeshift housing.

trade wind: A wind that almost always blows in one direction.

tropical: A region or climate that is frost free with temperatures high enough to support year-round plant growth.

West Indies: A name for the islands in the Atlantic Ocean between North and South America.

Pronunciation Guide*

akee	AH-kee
algae	AL-jee
Anancy	ah-NAHN-see
Arawak	AIR-uh-wahk
Ashanti	ah-SHAN-tee
bauxite	BAHK-site
boonoonoonoos	boo-NOO-noo-noos
cho, mon	CHOH mahn
cockroach no bidness in a fowl yard	CAHK-rohch no BID-ness in ah FOHL yahd
come gimme ya	come GIM-mee yah
cool runnings	KOOL RON-nings
deggeday	day-guh-DAY
epaulet	eh-peh-LEHT
Ghana	GAH-nah
irie	EYE-ree
lama	LAH-mah
mek wi go	meck wee goh
mento	MEHN-toh
mon	MAHN
nyam	NEE-yahm
patois	PAT-wah
Rastafarian	rahs-tah-FAHR-ee-ahn
reggae	REH-gay
ska	SKAH
tenky	TAIN-kee
wakud	WAHK-gud
Xamayca	zah-MAY-kah
yea	YAH
zemi	zee-MEE

*All pronunciations are approximate.

Further Reading

Berry, James R. A Thief in the Village and Other Stories of Jamaica. New York: Viking, 1990.

Hanson, Regina. The Tangerine Tree. New York: Clarion Books, 1995.

Hubley, John and Penny Hubley. A Family in Jamaica. Minneapolis: Lerner Publications Company, 1985.

Jamaica in Pictures. Minneapolis: Lerner Publications Company, 1997.

Kaufman, Cheryl Davidson. Cooking the Caribbean Way. Minneapolis: Lerner Publications Company, 1988.

Lincoln, Margarette. The Pirate's Handbook: How to Become a Rogue of the High Seas. New York: Cobblehill Books, 1995.

May, Chris. Bob Marley. London: Evans Brothers Ltd., 1985.

Sunk!: Exploring Underwater Archaeology. Minneapolis: Runestone Press, 1994.

Metric Conversion Chart

WHEN YOU KNOW:	MULTIPLY BY:	TO FIND:
teaspoon	5.0	milliliters
Tablespoon	15.0	milliliters
cup	0.24	liters
inches	2.54	centimeters
feet	0.3048	meters
miles	1.609	kilometers
square miles	2.59	square kilometers
degrees Fahrenheit	5/9 (after subtracting 32)	degrees Celsius

Index